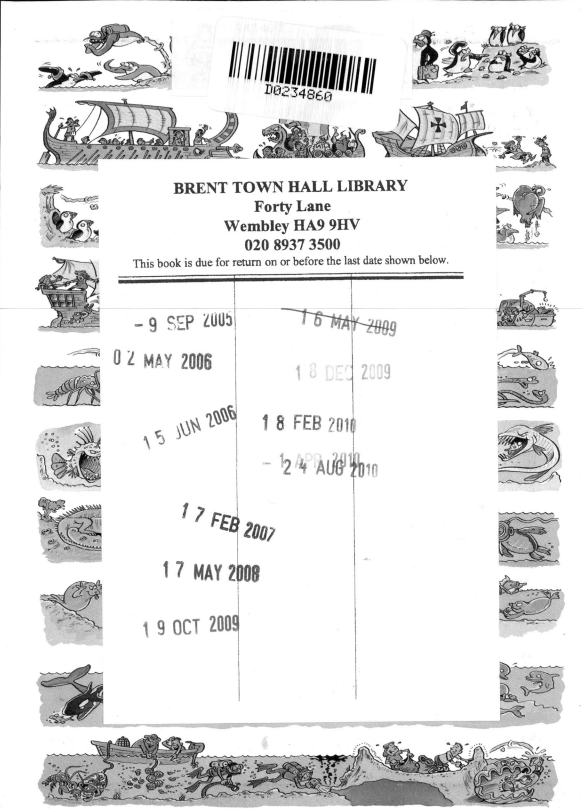

100

things you should know about

OCEANS

100

things you should know about

OCEANS

Clare Oliver

Consultant: Clive Carpenter

Miles Kelly PUBLISHING

First published in 2005 by
Miles Kelly Publishing Ltd
Bardfield Centre, Great Bardfield, Essex, CM7 4SL

2 4 6 8 10 9 7 5 3 1

Publishing Director: Anne Marshall
Project Management: Belinda Gallagher
Assistant Editors: Nicola Jessop, Nicola Sail
Designer: John Christopher, White Design
Artwork Commissioning: Lesley Cartlidge
Proofreader and Indexer: Lynn Bresler

ISBN 1-84236-352-2

Printed in China

British Library Cataloguing-in-Publication Data
A catalogue record for this book is available from the
British Library

ACKNOWLEDGEMENTS
The publishers would like to thank the following artists who have
contributed to this book:

Kuo Kang Chen
Peter Dennis
Richard Draper
Nicholas Forder
Chris Forsey
Terry Gabbey
Studio Galante
Alan Harris

Kevin Maddison
Janos Marffy
Alan Male
Steve Roberts
Martin Sanders
Mike Saunders
Gwen Tourret
Rudi Vizi

Cartoons by Mark Davis at Mackerel

www.mileskelly.net
info@mileskelly.net

Contents

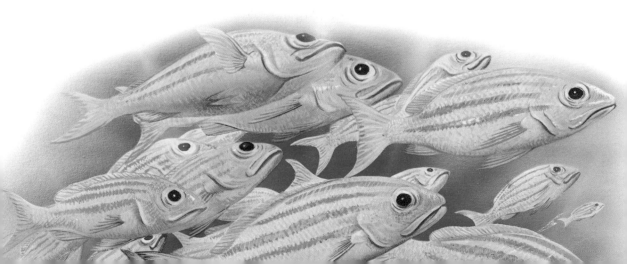

Water world

1 **Oceans cover over two-thirds of the Earth's rocky surface.** Their total area is about 362 million square kilometres, which means there is more than twice as much ocean as land! Although all the oceans flow into each other, we know them as four different oceans – the Pacific, Atlantic, Indian and Arctic. Our landmasses, the continents, rise out of the oceans.

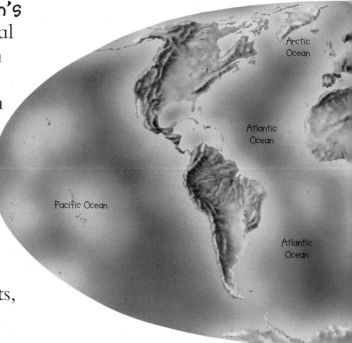

Arctic Ocean

Atlantic Ocean

Pacific Ocean

Atlantic Ocean

2 **The largest, deepest ocean is the Pacific.** It covers nearly half of our planet and is almost as big as the other three oceans put together! In places, the Pacific is so deep that the Earth's tallest mountain, Everest, would sink without a trace.

The deepest parts of the Pacific would cover Mount Everest without trace

▶ Mount Everest is the highest point on Earth, rising to 8848 metres. Parts of the Pacific Ocean are deeper than 10,000 metres.

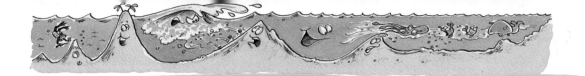

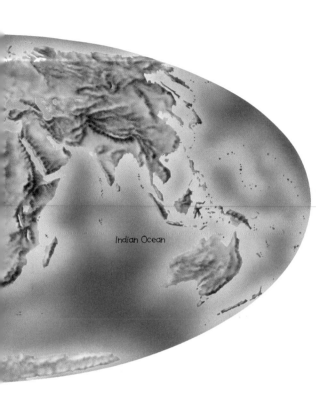

Indian Ocean

▲ The world's oceans cover most of our planet. Each ocean is made up of smaller bodies of water called seas.

Light hits the surface of the water

▶ A cup of sea water appears see-through. It is only when you look at a large area of sea that it has colour.

Scattered blue and green

3 **Oceans can look blue, green or grey.** This is because of the way light hits the surface. Water soaks up the red parts of light but scatters the blue-green parts, making the sea look different shades of blue or green.

4 **Seas can be red or dead.** A sea is a small part of an ocean. The Red Sea, for example, is the part of the Indian Ocean between Egypt and Saudi Arabia. Asia's Dead Sea isn't a true sea, but a landlocked lake. We call it a sea because it is a large body of water.

5 **There are streams in the oceans.** All the water in the oceans is constantly moving, but in some places it flows as currents, which take particular paths. One of these is the warm Gulf Stream, that travels around the edge of the Atlantic Ocean.

I DON'T BELIEVE IT!
97 percent of the world's water is in the oceans. Just a fraction is in freshwater lakes and rivers.

Ocean features

6 There are plains, mountains and valleys under the oceans, in areas called basins. Each basin has a rim (the flat continental shelf that meets the shore) and sides (the continental slope that drops away from the shelf). In the ocean basin there are flat abyssal plains, steep hills, huge underwater volcanoes called seamounts, and deep valleys called trenches.

▼ Magma (molten rock) escapes from the seabed to form a ridge. This ridge has collapsed to form a rift valley.

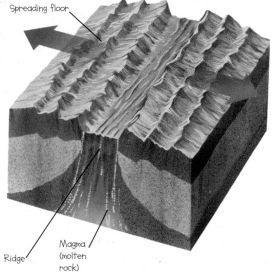

Spreading floor

Ridge

Magma (molten rock)

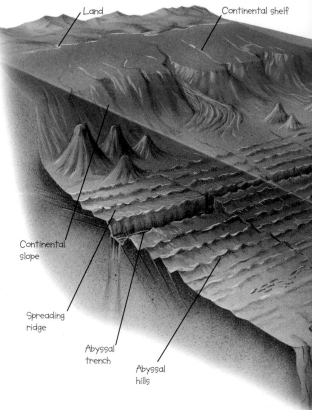

Land

Continental shelf

Continental slope

Spreading ridge

Abyssal trench

Abyssal hills

▲ Under the oceans there is a landscape similar to that found on land.

7 The ocean floor is spreading. Molten (liquid) rock inside the Earth seeps from holes on the seabed. As the rock cools, it forms new sections of floor that creep slowly out. Scientists have proved this fact by looking at layers of rock on the ocean floor. There are matching stripes of rock either side of a ridge. Each pair came from the same hot rock eruption, then slowly spread out.

Sea mount

Volcanic island

▼ An atoll is a ring—shaped coral reef that encloses a deep lagoon. It can form when a volcanic island sinks underwater.

1. Coral starts to grow

4. Coral atoll is left behind

2. Lagoon appears around volcano

3. Volcano disappears

Ocean trench

8 **Some islands are swallowed by the ocean.** Sometimes, a ring-shaped coral reef called an atoll marks where an island once was. The coral reef built up around the island. After the volcano blew its top, the reef remained.

▶ There are more Hawaiian islands still to come – Loihi is just visible beneath the water's surface.

I DON'T BELIEVE IT!
The world's longest mountain chain is under the ocean. It is the Mid—Ocean range and stretches around the middle of the Earth.

9 **New islands are born all the time.** When an underwater volcano erupts, its lava cools in the water. Layers of lava build up, and the volcano grows in size. Eventually, it is tall enough to peep above the waves. The Hawaiian islands rose from the sea like this.

Tides and shores

10 **The sea level rises and falls twice each day along the coast.** This is known as high and low tides. Tides happen because of the pull of the Moon, which lifts water from the part of the Earth's surface facing it.

▼ At high tide, the sea rises up the shore and dumps seaweed, shells and drift wood. Most coasts have two high tides and two low tides every day.

High tides happen at the same time each day on opposite sides of the Earth

At high tide the water level rises

At low tide the water level goes down again

11 **Spring tides are especially high.** They occur twice a month, when the Moon is in line with the Earth and the Sun. Then, the Sun's pulling force joins the Moon's and seawater is lifted higher than usual. The opposite happens when the Moon and Sun are at right angles to the Earth. Then, their pulling powers work against each other causing weak neap tides – the lowest high tides and low tides.

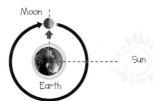

Moon

Sun

Earth

◀ Neap tides occur when the Sun and Moon are at right angles to each other and pulling in different directions.

Earth

Sun

Moon

▶ Spring tides occur when the Sun and the Moon are lined up and pulling together.

12 **The sea is strong enough to carve into rock.** Pounding waves batter coastlines and erode, or wear away, the rock.

▼ Waves can create amazing shapes such as pillars called sea stacks.

Sea stack

Arch

▲ A tsunami can travel faster than a jumbo jet.

15 **Tidal waves are the most powerful waves.** Also known as tsunamis, they happen when underwater earthquakes trigger tremendous shock waves. These whip up a wall of water that travels across the sea's surface.

13 **Sand is found on bars and spits, as well as beaches.** It is made up of grains of worn-down rock and shell. Sand collects on shorelines and spits, but also forms on offshore beaches called sand bars. Spits are narrow ridges of worn sand and pebbles.

I DON'T BELIEVE IT!
The biggest tsunami was taller than five Statues of Liberty! It hit the Japanese Ryuku Islands in 1771.

14 **Some shores are swampy.** This makes the border between land and sea hard to pinpoint. Muddy coastlines include tropical mangrove swamps that are flooded by salty water from the sea.

▶ The stilt-like roots of mangrove trees take in both air and water.

Life in a rock pool

16 Rock pools are teeming with all kinds of creatures. Limpets are a kind of shellfish. They live on rocks and in pools at shorelines. Here, they eat slimy, green algae, but they have to withstand the crashing tide. They cling to the rock with their muscular foot, only moving when the tide is out.

17 Some anemones fight with harpoons. Beadlet anemones will sometimes fight over a feeding ground. Their weapon is the poison they usually use to stun their prey. They shoot tiny hooks like harpoons at each other until the weakest one gives in.

▲ Anemones are named after flowers, because of their petal-like arms.

18 Starfish can grow new arms. They may have as many as 40 arms, or rays. If a predator grabs hold of one, the starfish abandons the ray, and uses the others to make its getaway!

◄ Starfish are relatives of brittle stars, sea urchins and sea cucumbers.

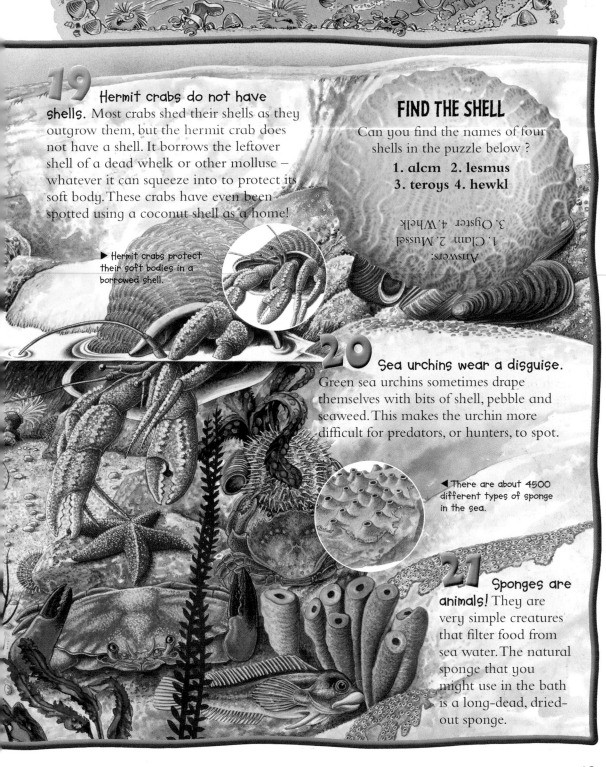

19 **Hermit crabs do not have shells.** Most crabs shed their shells as they outgrow them, but the hermit crab does not have a shell. It borrows the leftover shell of a dead whelk or other mollusc – whatever it can squeeze into to protect its soft body. These crabs have even been spotted using a coconut shell as a home!

▶ Hermit crabs protect their soft bodies in a borrowed shell.

FIND THE SHELL

Can you find the names of four shells in the puzzle below ?

1. alcm   2. lesmus
3. teroys   4. hewkl

Answers:
1. Clam 2. Mussel
3. Oyster 4. Whelk

20 **Sea urchins wear a disguise.** Green sea urchins sometimes drape themselves with bits of shell, pebble and seaweed. This makes the urchin more difficult for predators, or hunters, to spot.

◀ There are about 4500 different types of sponge in the sea.

21 **Sponges are animals!** They are very simple creatures that filter food from sea water. The natural sponge that you might use in the bath is a long-dead, dried-out sponge.

13

Colourful coral

22 **Tiny animals build huge underwater walls.** These are built up from coral, the leftover skeletons of sea creatures called polyps. Over millions of years, enough skeletons pile up to form huge, wall-like structures called reefs. Coral reefs are full of hidey-holes and make brilliant habitats for all sorts of amazing, colourful sea life.

23 **The world's biggest shellfish lives on coral reefs.** Giant clams grow to well over one metre long – big enough for you to bathe in its shell!

24 **Seahorse dads have the babies.** They don't exactly give birth, but they store the eggs in a pouch on their belly. When the eggs are ready to hatch, a stream of miniature seahorses billows out from the dad's pouch.

▶ Baby seahorses stream out of their father's pouch and into the sea.

Parrot fish

Giant clam

Clownfish

25 **Some fish go to the cleaners.**
Cleaner wrasse are little fish that are paid for
cleaning! Larger fish, such as groupers and
moray eels visit the wrasse, which nibble all the
parasites and other bits of dirt off the bigger
fishes' bodies – what a feast!

26 **Clownfish are sting-proof.** Most
creatures steer clear of an anemone's stinging
tentacles. But the clownfish swims among the
stingers, where it's safe from predators. Strangely,
the anemone doesn't seem to sting the clownfish.

**I DON'T
BELIEVE IT!**
You can see the Great
Barrier Reef from space! At
over 2000 km long, it is the
largest structure ever built
by living creatures.

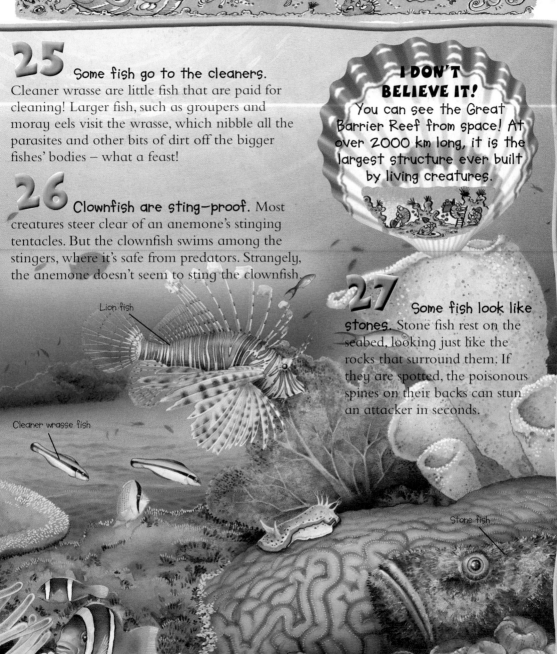

Lion fish

Cleaner wrasse fish

27 **Some fish look like
stones.** Stone fish rest on the
seabed, looking just like the
rocks that surround them. If
they are spotted, the poisonous
spines on their backs can stun
an attacker in seconds.

Stone fish

▲ Tropical coral reefs are the
habitat of an amazing range of
marine plants and creatures.

Swimming machines

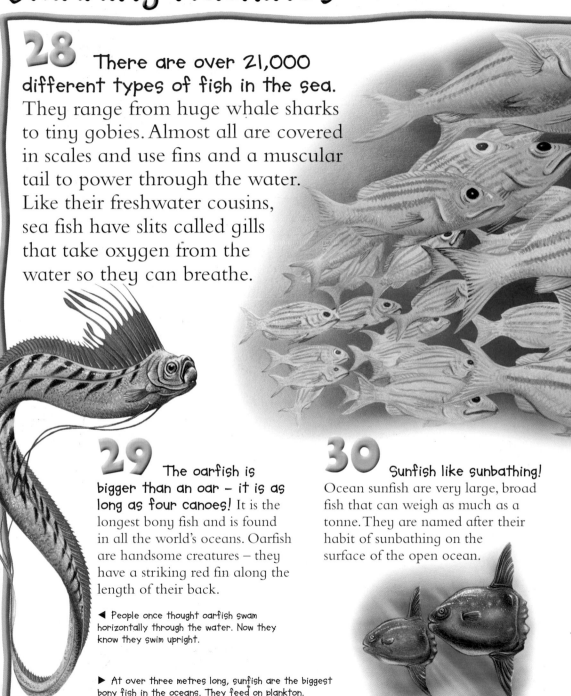

28 There are over 21,000 different types of fish in the sea. They range from huge whale sharks to tiny gobies. Almost all are covered in scales and use fins and a muscular tail to power through the water. Like their freshwater cousins, sea fish have slits called gills that take oxygen from the water so they can breathe.

29 The oarfish is bigger than an oar – it is as long as four canoes! It is the longest bony fish and is found in all the world's oceans. Oarfish are handsome creatures – they have a striking red fin along the length of their back.

◀ People once thought oarfish swam horizontally through the water. Now they know they swim upright.

30 Sunfish like sunbathing! Ocean sunfish are very large, broad fish that can weigh as much as a tonne. They are named after their habit of sunbathing on the surface of the open ocean.

▶ At over three metres long, sunfish are the biggest bony fish in the oceans. They feed on plankton.

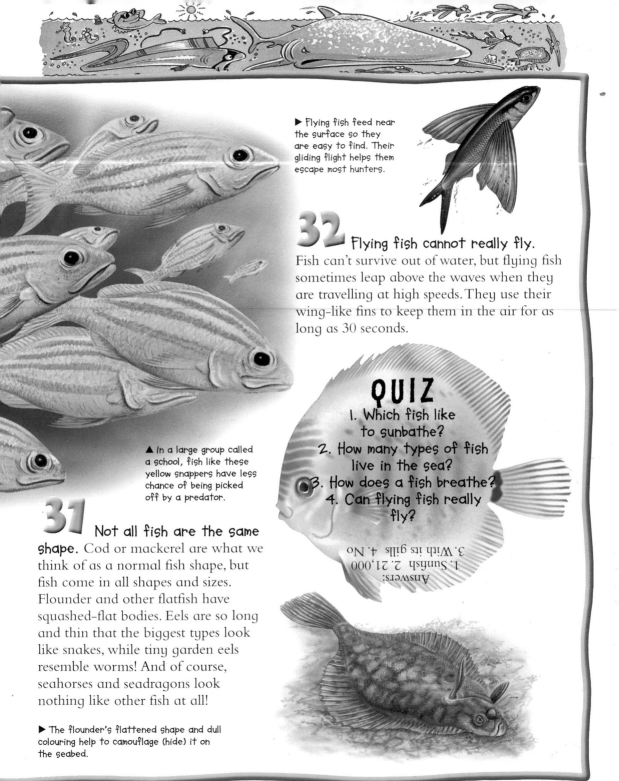

▶ Flying fish feed near the surface so they are easy to find. Their gliding flight helps them escape most hunters.

32 Flying fish cannot really fly.

Fish can't survive out of water, but flying fish sometimes leap above the waves when they are travelling at high speeds. They use their wing-like fins to keep them in the air for as long as 30 seconds.

▲ In a large group called a school, fish like these yellow snappers have less chance of being picked off by a predator.

31 Not all fish are the same shape.

Cod or mackerel are what we think of as a normal fish shape, but fish come in all shapes and sizes. Flounder and other flatfish have squashed-flat bodies. Eels are so long and thin that the biggest types look like snakes, while tiny garden eels resemble worms! And of course, seahorses and seadragons look nothing like other fish at all!

▶ The flounder's flattened shape and dull colouring help to camouflage (hide) it on the seabed.

QUIZ

1. Which fish like to sunbathe?
2. How many types of fish live in the sea?
3. How does a fish breathe?
4. Can flying fish really fly?

Answers:
1. Sunfish 2. 21,000 3. With its gills 4. No

Shark!

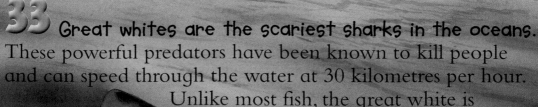

33 Great whites are the scariest sharks in the oceans. These powerful predators have been known to kill people and can speed through the water at 30 kilometres per hour. Unlike most fish, the great white is warm-blooded. This allows its muscles to work well, but also means the shark has to feed on plenty of meat.

▼ Basking sharks eat enormous amounts of plankton. They sieve through around 1000 tonnes of water every hour.

▲ Great white sharks are fierce hunters. They will attack and eat almost anything, but prefer to feed on seals.

34 Most sharks are meat-eaters. Herring are a favourite food for sand tiger and thresher sharks, while a hungry tiger shark will gobble up just about anything! Strangely, some of the biggest sharks take the smallest prey. Whale sharks and basking sharks eat tiny sea creatures called plankton.

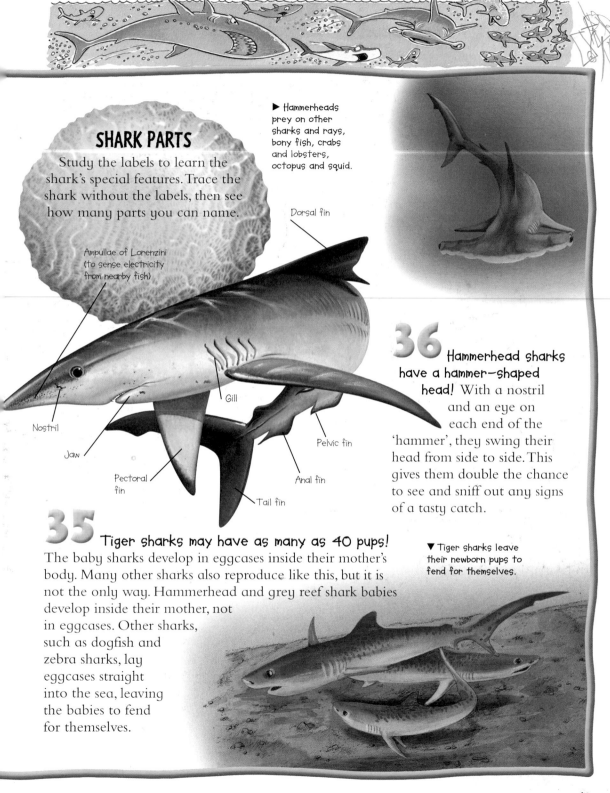

SHARK PARTS

Study the labels to learn the shark's special features. Trace the shark without the labels, then see how many parts you can name.

► Hammerheads prey on other sharks and rays, bony fish, crabs and lobsters, octopus and squid.

Ampullae of Lorenzini (to sense electricity from nearby fish)

Dorsal fin

Nostril

Jaw

Pectoral fin

Gill

Pelvic fin

Anal fin

Tail fin

36 Hammerhead sharks have a hammer–shaped head! With a nostril and an eye on each end of the 'hammer', they swing their head from side to side. This gives them double the chance to see and sniff out any signs of a tasty catch.

35 Tiger sharks may have as many as 40 pups! The baby sharks develop in eggcases inside their mother's body. Many other sharks also reproduce like this, but it is not the only way. Hammerhead and grey reef shark babies develop inside their mother, not in eggcases. Other sharks, such as dogfish and zebra sharks, lay eggcases straight into the sea, leaving the babies to fend for themselves.

▼ Tiger sharks leave their newborn pups to fend for themselves.

Whales and dolphins

37 The biggest animal on the planet lives in the oceans. It is the blue whale, measuring about 28 metres in length and weighing up to 190 tonnes. It feeds by filtering tiny, shrimp-like creatures called krill from the water – about four tonnes of krill a day! Like other great whales, it has special, sieve-like parts in its mouth called baleen plates.

▲ As the sperm whale surfaces, it pushes out stale air through its blowhole. It fills its lungs with fresh air and dives down again.

38 Whales and dolphins have to come to the surface for air. This is because they are mammals, like we are. Sperm whales hold their breath the longest. They have been known to stay underwater for nearly two hours.

▲ Blue whale calves feed on their mother's rich milk until they are around eight months old.

41 **Killer whales play with their food.** They especially like to catch baby seals, which they toss into the air before eating. Killer whales are not true whales, but the largest dolphins. They have teeth for chewing, instead of baleen plates.

▲ Killer whales carry the baby seals out to sea before eating them.

▶ The beluga is a type of white whale. It makes a range of noises – whistles, clangs, chirps and moos!

39 **Dolphins and whales sing songs to communicate.** The noisiest is the humpback whale, whose wailing noises can be heard for hundreds of kilometres. The sweetest is the beluga – nicknamed the 'sea canary'. Songs are used to attract a mate, or just to keep track of each other.

42 **Moby Dick was a famous white whale.** It starred in a book by Herman Melville about a white sperm whale and a whaler called Captain Ahab.

40 **The narwhal has a horn like a unicorn's.** This Arctic whale has a long, twirly tooth that spirals out of its head. The males use their tusks as a weapon when they are fighting over females.

I DON'T BELIEVE IT!
Barnacles are shellfish. They attach themselves to ships' hulls, or the bodies of grey whales and other large sea animals.

▲ The narwhal's three-metre tusk seems too long for its body.

Sleek swimmers

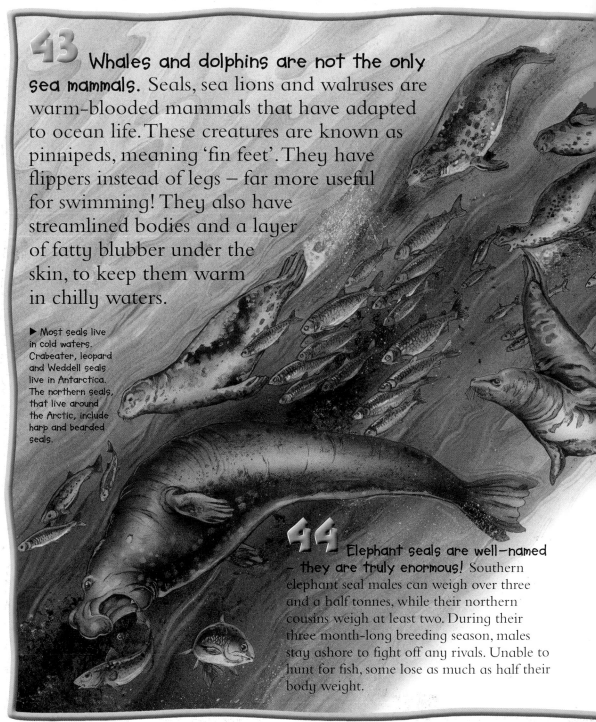

43 **Whales and dolphins are not the only sea mammals.** Seals, sea lions and walruses are warm-blooded mammals that have adapted to ocean life. These creatures are known as pinnipeds, meaning 'fin feet'. They have flippers instead of legs – far more useful for swimming! They also have streamlined bodies and a layer of fatty blubber under the skin, to keep them warm in chilly waters.

▶ Most seals live in cold waters. Crabeater, leopard and Weddell seals live in Antarctica. The northern seals, that live around the Arctic, include harp and bearded seals.

44 **Elephant seals are well-named – they are truly enormous!** Southern elephant seal males can weigh over three and a half tonnes, while their northern cousins weigh at least two. During their three month-long breeding season, males stay ashore to fight off any rivals. Unable to hunt for fish, some lose as much as half their body weight.

46 Sea otters anchor themselves when they sleep. These playful creatures live off the Pacific coast among huge forests of giant seaweed called kelp. When they take a snooze, they wrap a strand of kelp around their body to stop them being washed out to sea.

▲ Anchored to the kelp, a sea otter is free to crack open a crab shell – and snack!

45 Walruses seem to change colour! When a walrus is in the water, it appears pale brown or even white. This is because blood drains from the skin's surface to stop the body losing heat. On land, the blood returns to the skin and walruses can look reddish brown or pink!

▼ Walruses use their tusks as weapons. They are also used to break breathing holes in the ice, and to help the walrus pull itself out of the water.

I DON'T BELIEVE IT!
Leopard seals sing in their sleep! These seals, found in the Antarctic, chirp and whistle while they snooze.

Ocean reptiles

47 **Marine iguanas are the most seaworthy lizards.** Most lizards prefer life on land, where it is easier to warm up their cold-blooded bodies, but marine iguanas depend on the sea for their food. They dive underwater to graze on the algae and seaweed growing on rocks.

▲ Marine iguanas are found around the Galapagos Islands in the Pacific. When they are not diving for food, they bask on the rocks that dot the island coastlines. The lizards' dark skin helps to absorb the Sun's heat.

48 **Turtles come ashore only to lay their eggs.** Although they are born on land, turtles head for the sea the minute they hatch. Females return to the beach where they were born to dig their nest. After they have laid their eggs, they go straight back to the water. Hawksbill turtles may lay up to 140 eggs in a clutch, while some green turtle females clock up 800 eggs in a year!

▲ In a single breeding season, a female green turtle may lay as many as ten clutches, each containing up to 80 eggs!

49

There are venomous (poisonous) snakes in the sea. Most stay close to land and come ashore to lay their eggs. Banded sea snakes, for example, cruise around coral reefs in search of their favourite food, eels. But the yellow-bellied sea snake never leaves the water. It gives birth to live babies in the open ocean.

▼ Banded sea snakes use venom (poison) to stun prey, but the yellow-bellied sea snake has a sneakier trick. Once its colourful underside has attracted some fish, it darts back – so the fish are next to its open mouth! The venom of sea snakes is more powerful than that of any land snake.

Banded sea snake

Yellow–bellied sea snake

MIX AND MATCH

Can you match these sea turtles to their names?

1. Green 2. Hawksbill
3. Leatherback 4. Loggerhead

Answers:
1C 2B 3D 4A

a.

b.

c.

d.

▼ Leatherbacks are the biggest turtles in the world and can grow to four metres in length.

50

Leatherbacks dive up to 1200 metres for dinner. These turtles hold the record for being the biggest sea turtles and for making the deepest dives. Leatherbacks feed mostly on jellyfish but their diet also includes molluscs, crabs and lobsters, starfish and sea urchins.

Icy depths

51 Few creatures can survive in the dark, icy-cold ocean depths. Food is so hard to come by, the deep-sea anglerfish does not waste energy chasing prey – it has developed a clever fishing trick. A stringy 'fishing rod' with a glowing tip extends from its dorsal fin or hangs above its jaw. This attracts smaller fish to the anglerfish's big mouth.

▼ Anglerfish are black or brown for camouflage. Only their glowing 'fishing rod' is visible in the gloom.

▼ The light created by deep-sea fish, or by bacteria living on their bodies, is known as biological light, or bioluminescence.

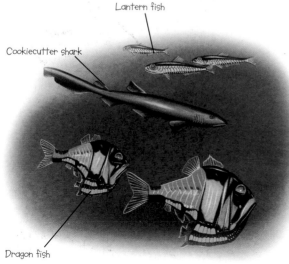

Lantern fish

Cookiecutter shark

Dragon fish

52 Some deep-sea fish glow in the dark. As well as tempting prey, light also confuses predators. About 1500 different deep-sea fish give off light. The lantern fish's whole body glows, while the dragon fish has light organs dotted along its sides and belly. Just the belly of the cookiecutter shark gives off a ghostly glow. Cookiecutters take biscuit-shaped bites out of their prey's body!

53 **Black swallowers are real greedy-guts!** These strange fish are just 25 centimetres long but can eat fish far bigger than themselves. Their loose jaws unhinge to fit over the prey. Then the stretchy body expands to take in their enormous meal.

▼ Like many deep-sea fish, black swallowers have smooth, scaleless skin.

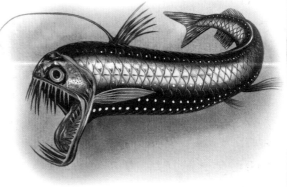

▲ The viperfish is named for its long, snake-like fangs.

54 **Viperfish have teeth which are invisible in the dark.** They swim around with their jaws wide open. Deep-sea shrimp often see nothing until they are right inside the viperfish's mouth.

▶ Tubeworms grow around deep-sea volcanoes called black smokers.

I DON'T BELIEVE IT!
Female deep-sea anglerfish grow to 120 centimetres in length, but the males are a tiny six centimetres!

55 **On the seabed, there are worms as long as cars!** These are giant tubeworms and they cluster around hot spots on the ocean floor. They feed on tiny particles that they filter from the water.

Amazing journeys

56 Many ocean animals travel incredible distances. Spiny lobsters spend the summer feeding off the coast of Florida, but head south in autumn to deeper waters. They travel about 50 kilometres along the seabed, in columns that may be more than 50-strong. They keep together by touch, using their long, spiky antennae (feelers).

▲ In spring, spiny lobsters return to shallower waters. They spawn (lay their eggs) around the coral reefs off the Straits of Florida.

57 Arctic terns are the long-distance flying champs. These seabirds fly farther than any other bird. After nesting in the Arctic, they head south for the Antarctic. In its lifetime, one bird might cover more than 1,250,000 kilometres!

◀ In a single year, an Arctic tern may fly more than 40,000 kilometres!

58 Grey whales migrate, or travel, farther than any other mammal. There are two main grey whale populations in the Pacific. One spends summer off the Alaskan coast. In winter they migrate south to Mexico to breed. The whales may swim nearly 20,000 kilometres in a year. The other grey whale group spends summer off the coast of Russia, then travels south to Korea.

▶ Grey whales spend summer in the Bering Sea, feeding on tiny, shrimp–like creatures called amphipods. They spend their breeding season, December to March, in the warmer waters off Mexico.

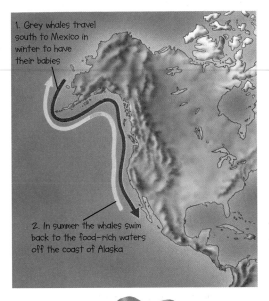

1. Grey whales travel south to Mexico in winter to have their babies

2. In summer the whales swim back to the food-rich waters off the coast of Alaska

59 Baby loggerhead turtles make a two–year journey. They are born on beaches in Japan. The hatchlings hurry down to the sea and set off across the Pacific to Mexico, a journey of 10,000 kilometres. They spend about five years there before returning to Japan to breed.

▼ Not all loggerhead hatchlings make it to the sea. As they race down the beach, some are picked off by hungry gulls or crabs.

I DON'T BELIEVE IT!
Eels and salmon swim thousands of kilometres from the sea to spawn in the same river nurseries where they were born.

On the wing

60 **Wandering albatrosses are the biggest seabirds.** An albatross has a wingspan of around three metres – about the length of a family car! These sea birds are so large, they take off by launching from a cliff. Albatrosses spend months at sea. They are such expert gliders that they even sleep on the wing. To feed, they land on the sea, where they sit and catch creatures such as squid.

▶ A gannet dives and captures a fishy meal in its beak.

61 **Gannets wear air–bag shock absorbers.** The gannet's feeding technique is to plummet headfirst into the ocean and catch a fish in its beak. It dives at high-speed and hits the water hard. Luckily, the gannet's head is protected with sacs of air that absorb most of the shock.

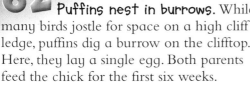

62 **Puffins nest in burrows.** While many birds jostle for space on a high cliff ledge, puffins dig a burrow on the clifftop. Here, they lay a single egg. Both parents feed the chick for the first six weeks.

▼ Puffins often scrape their own burrows, or they may take over an abandoned rabbit hole.

64 **Boobies dance to attract a mate.** There are two types of booby, blue or red-footed. The dancing draws attention to the male's colourful feet. Perhaps this stops the females from mating with the wrong type of bird.

▼ Boobies are tropical seabirds that nest in colonies.

63 **Frigate birds puff up a balloon for their mate.** Male frigate birds have a bright-red pouch on their throat. They inflate, or blow up, the pouch as part of their display to attract a female.

▲ A frigate bird shows off to its mate.

Perfect penguins

65 **Macaroni, chinstrap, jackass and emperor are all types of penguin.** There are 17 different types in total, and most live around the Antarctic. Penguins feed on fish, squid and krill. Their black-and-white plumage is important camouflage. Seen from above, a penguin's black back blends in with the water. The white belly is hard to distinguish from the sunlit surface of the sea.

Chinstrap penguin

66 **Penguins can swim, but not fly.** They have oily, waterproofed feathers and flipper-like wings. Instead of lightweight, hollow bones – like a flying bird's – some penguins have solid, heavy bones. This enables them to stay underwater longer when diving for food. Emperor penguins can stay under for 15 minutes or more.

I DON'T BELIEVE IT!
The fastest swimming bird is the gentoo penguin. It has been known to swim at speeds of 27 kilometres per hour!

▶ Penguins have a layer of fat under their feathers to protect them in the icy water.

Gentoo penguin

Adélie penguin

King penguin

Emperor penguin

67
Emperor penguin dads balance an egg on their feet. They do this to keep their egg off the Antarctic ice, where it would freeze. The female leaves her mate with the egg for the whole two months that it takes to hatch. The male has to go without food during this time. When the chick hatches, the mother returns and both parents help to raise it.

▶ A downy emperor penguin chick cannot find its own food in the sea. It must wait until it has grown its waterproof, adult plumage.

▲ An Adélie penguin builds its nest from stones and small rocks.

68
Some penguins build stone circles. This is the way that Adélie and gentoo penguins build nests on the shingled shores where they breed. First, they scrape out a small dip with their flippered feet and then they surround the hollow with a circle of pebbles.

Harvests from the sea

◀ Fishermen attach buoys to their lobster pots, so they can remember where to find them again.

69 **Oysters come from beds – and lobsters from pots!** The animals in the oceans feed other sea creatures, and they feed us, too! To gather oysters, fishermen raise them on trays or poles in the water. First, they collect oyster larvae, or babies. They attract them by putting out sticks hung with shells. Lobster larvae are too difficult to collect, but the adults are caught in pots filled with fish bait.

70 **Some farmers grow seaweed.** Seaweed is delicious to eat, and is also a useful ingredient in products such as ice cream and plant fertilizer. In shallow, tropical waters, people grow their own on plots of seabed.

▲ The harvested seaweed can be dried in the sun to preserve it.

▶ The oil platform's welded–steel legs rest on the seabed. They support the platform around 15 metres above the surface of the water.

Flare

Crane

Derrick

Helicopter landing pad

Oil processing area

71
Sea minerals are big business. Minerals are useful substances that we mine from the ground – and oceans are full of them! The most valuable are oil and gas, which are pumped from the seabed and piped ashore or transported in huge supertankers. Salt is another important mineral. In hot, low-lying areas, people build walls to hold shallow pools of sea water. The water dries up in the sun, leaving behind crystals of salt.

72
There are gemstones under the sea. Pearls are made by oysters. If a grain of sand is lodged inside an oyster's shell, it irritates its soft body. The oyster coats the sand with a substance called nacre, which is also used to line the inside of the shell. Over the years, more nacre builds up and the pearl gets bigger.

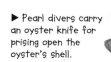

QUIZ
1. What are the young of lobster called?
2. What substances are pumped from the seabed?
3. Is seaweed edible?
4. Which gemstone is made by oysters?

Answers:
1. Larvae 2. Oil and gas
3. Yes 4. Pearl

▶ Pearl divers carry an oyster knife for prising open the oyster's shell.

First voyages

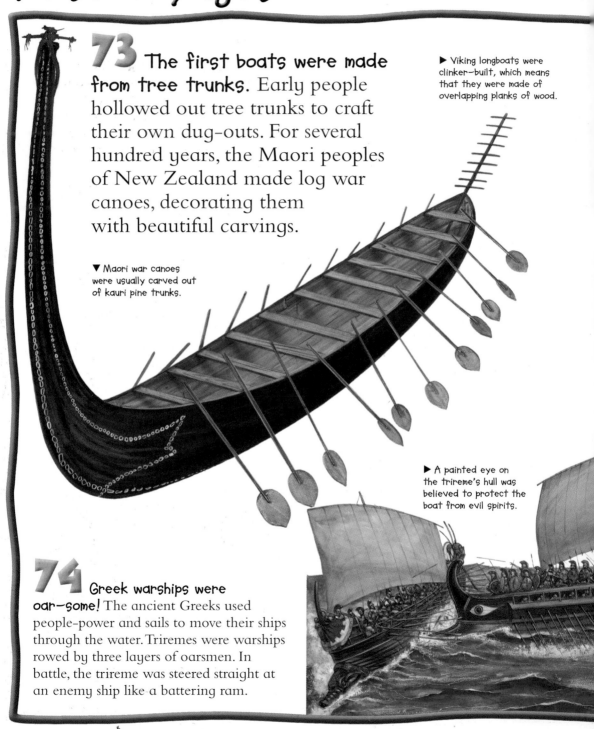

73 **The first boats were made from tree trunks.** Early people hollowed out tree trunks to craft their own dug-outs. For several hundred years, the Maori peoples of New Zealand made log war canoes, decorating them with beautiful carvings.

▶ Viking longboats were clinker—built, which means that they were made of overlapping planks of wood.

▼ Maori war canoes were usually carved out of kauri pine trunks.

▶ A painted eye on the trireme's hull was believed to protect the boat from evil spirits.

74 **Greek warships were oar—some!** The ancient Greeks used people-power and sails to move their ships through the water. Triremes were warships rowed by three layers of oarsmen. In battle, the trireme was steered straight at an enemy ship like a battering ram.

77 Boats found the way to a new world. The 1400s were an amazing time of exploration and discovery. One explorer, Christopher Columbus, set sail from Spain in 1492 with a fleet of three ships. He hoped to find a new trade route to India, but instead he found the Americas! Before then, they were not even on the map!

▶ Columbus's fleet consisted of the *Niña*, the *Pinta* and the *Santa Maria*.

75 Dragons guarded Viking longboats. Scandinavian seafarers decorated their boats' prows with carvings of dragons and serpents to terrify their enemies. Built from overlapping planks, Viking longboats were very seaworthy. Leif Ericson was the first Viking to cross the Atlantic Ocean to Newfoundland, in North America just over 1000 years ago.

76 It is thought that Chinese navigators made the first compass—like device about 2500 years ago. Compasses use the Earth's magnetism to show the directions of north, south, east and west. They are used at sea, where there are no landmarks. The navigators used lodestone, a naturally magnetic rock, to magnetize the needle.

▶ Early compasses were very simple. During the 1300s compasses became more detailed.

BOAT SCRAMBLE!
Unscramble the letters to find the names of six different types of boat.

1. leacvar 2. chenroos
3. rarlewt 4. coclear
5. leglay 6. pecpril

Answers:
1. Caravel 2. Schooner
3. Trawler 4. Coracle
5. Galley 6. Clipper

Pirates!

78 **Pirates once ruled the high seas.**
Pirates are sailors who attack and board
other ships to steal their cargoes.
Their golden age was during the
1600s and 1700s. This was when
heavily laden ships carried
treasures, weapons and goods
back to Europe from colonies
in the Americas, Africa and
Asia. Edward Teach, better
known as Blackbeard, was
one of the most terrifying
pirates. He attacked ships
off the coast of North
America during the early
1700s. To frighten his
victims, it is said that he
used to set fire to his
own beard!

▼ Pirate weapons had often
been stolen on previous raids.
The men fought to the death.

79 **There were women
pirates, too.** Piracy was a man's
world, but some women also took to
the high seas. Mary Read and Anne
Bonny were part of a pirate crew
sailing around the Caribbean. They
wore men's clothes and used fighting
weapons, including daggers, cutlasses
and pistols.

80
There are still pirates on the oceans. Despite police patrols who watch for pirates and smugglers, a few pirates still operate. Luxury yachts are an easy target and in the South China Sea, pirate gangs on motor boats even attack large merchant ships.

▼ Divers have found some extraordinary hoards of treasure on board sunken galleons.

81
There is treasure lying under the sea. Over the centuries, many ships sunk in storms or hit reefs. They include pirate ships loaded with stolen booty. Some ships were deliberately sunk by pirates. The bed of the Caribbean Sea is littered with the remains of Spanish galleons, many of which still hold treasure!

PIRATE FLAG!
You will need:
paper   paints   brushes
The skull-and-crossbones is the most famous pirate flag, but it was not the only one. Copy one of these designs!

Going under

82 **A submarine has dived deeper than 10,000 metres.** The two-person *Trieste* made history in 1960 in an expedition to the Mariana Trench in the Pacific, the deepest part of any ocean. It took the submarine five hours to reach the bottom, a distance of 10,911 metres. On the way down, the extreme water pressure cracked part of the craft, but luckily, the two men inside returned to the surface unharmed.

▲ *Trieste* spent 20 minutes at the bottom of the Mariana Trench. The trench is so deep, you could stack the world's tallest building, the CN Tower, inside it 19 times (left)!

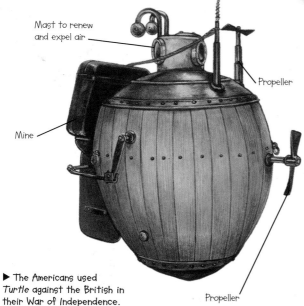

Mast to renew and expel air

Propeller

Mine

▶ The Americans used *Turtle* against the British in their War of Independence.

Propeller

83 **The first combat submarine was shaped like an egg!** *Turtle* was a one-person submarine that made its test dive in 1776. It was the first real submarine. It did not have an engine – it was driven by a propeller that was turned by hand! *Turtle* was built for war. It travelled just below the surface and could fix bombs to the bottom of enemy ships.

84

Divers have a spare pair of lungs. Scuba divers wear special breathing apparatus called 'aqua lungs'. French divers, Jacques Cousteau and Emile Gagnan, came up with the idea of a portable oxygen supply. This meant that divers were able to swim freely for the first time, rather than wearing a heavy suit and helmet.

I DON'T BELIEVE IT!
In 1963 Jacques Cousteau built a village on the bed of the Red Sea. Along with four other divers, he lived there for a whole month.

◄ Divers control their breathing to make their oxygen supply last as long as possible.

85

The biggest submarines weighed 26,500 tonnes. They were Russian submarines called *Typhoons*, built in the 1970s and 1980s. As well as being the biggest subs, they were also the fastest, able to top 40 knots.

Periscope

Rudder

Living quarters

Torpedo firing tube

Engine room

▲ The *Typhoons* did not need to come up to refuel because they were nuclear-powered.

Diving plane

41

Superboats

86 **Some ships are invisible.** Stealth warships are not really invisible, of course, but they are hard to detect using radar. There are already materials being used for ships that can absorb some radar signals. Some paints can soak up radar, too, and signals are also bounced off in confusing directions by the ships' strange, angled hulls.

I DON'T BELIEVE IT!
People said *Titanic* was unsinkable. But it hit an iceberg and sank on its maiden voyage. More than 1500 people drowned.

87 **The world's biggest ship is nearly half a kilometre long.** It is a supertanker called *Jahre Viking*. Supertankers carry cargoes of oil around the world. They move slowly because they are so huge and heavy.

▲ An angled, sloping hull gives very little radar echo. This makes the stealth ship's location hard to pinpoint.

▼ The giant supertanker *Jahre Viking* is just over 458 metres long.

88
Not all boats ride the waves. Hovercrafts sit slightly above the water. They have a rubbery skirt that traps a cushion of air for them to ride on. Without the drag of the water to work against, hovercraft can cross the water much faster.

◀ Hovercraft can travel at up to 65 knots, the equivalent of 120 kilometres per hour.

▼ *Freedom Ship* will be over 1300 metres long. Aircraft 'taxis' will be able to take off and land on its rooftop runway.

89
Ships can give piggy—backs!
Heavy-lift ships can sink part of their deck underwater, so a smaller ship can sail aboard for a free ride. Some ships carry planes. Aircraft carriers transport planes that are too small to carry enough fuel for long distances. The deck doubles up as a runway, where the planes take off and land.

90
***Freedom Ship* will resemble a floating city.** It will be one of the first ocean cities, with apartments, shopping centres, a school and a hospital. The people who live on *Freedom* will circle the Earth once every two years. By following the Sun, they will live in constant summertime!

Riding the waves

91 **The first sea sport was surfing.** It took off in the 1950s, but was invented centuries earlier in Hawaii. Hawaii is still one of the best places to surf – at Waimea Bay, surfers catch waves that are up to 11 metres high. The record for the longest rides, though, are made off the coast of Mexico, where it is possible to surf for more than one-and-a-half kilometres.

▶ Modern surfboards are made of super–light materials. This means they create little drag in the water – and the surfer can reach high speeds!

92 **A single boat towed 100 waterskiers!** This record was made off the coast of Australia in 1986 and no one has beaten it yet. The drag boat was a cruiser called *Reef Cat.*

◀ Water skiing is now one of the most popular of all water sports.

QUIZ
1. What was the name of the fastest hydroplane?
2. When did jetskis go on sale?
3. Where is Waimea Bay?
4. What is a trimaran?

Answers:
1. *Spirit of Australia* 2. 1973 3. Hawaii 4. A three-hulled boat

93 **Jetskiers can travel at nearly 100 kilometres per hour.** Jetskis were developed in the 1960s. Their inventor was an American called Clayton Jacobsen who wanted to combine his two favourite hobbies, motorbikes and waterskiing. Today, some jetskiers are professional sportspeople.

◀ Jetskis first went on sale in 1973.

◀ Trimarans have three hulls, while catamarans have two.

94 **Three hulls are sometimes better than one.** Powerboating is an exciting, dangerous sport. Competitors are always trying out new boat designs that will race even faster. Multi-hulled boats minimize drag, but keep the boat steady. Trimarans have three slender, streamlined hulls that cut through the water.

95 **Hydroplanes fly over the waves.** They are a cross between a boat and a plane. Special 'wings' raise the hull two metres above the water. The fastest hydroplane ever was *Spirit of Australia*. Driven by Kenneth Warby, it sped along at more than 500 kilometres per hour above the surface of the water!

▶ Hydroplanes are motor boats that skim across the surface of the water.

Ocean stories

▼ Jason and the Argonauts steer their ship between two huge moving cliffs called the Cyanean Rocks. They faced many dangers on their journey.

96 **The Greek hero Jason made an epic sea voyage.** The ancient Greeks made up lots of sea adventure stories, probably because they lived on scattered islands. In the legend of the Argonauts, a hero called Jason sets off in a boat called the *Argos* with a band of brave men. He goes on a quest to find the Golden Fleece, a precious sheepskin guarded by a fierce dragon.

97 **Neptune (or Poseidon) was an undersea god.** Poseidon was the name used by the ancient Greeks and Neptune by the ancient Romans. Both civilizations pictured their god with a fork called a trident. They blamed their gods for the terrible storms that wrecked boats in the Mediterranean.

▶ Neptune raises his trident and whips up a storm.

▲ The beautiful goddess Aphrodite emerges from the sea.

99 Long ago, people believed in a giant sea monster, called the kraken. The stories were used to explain the dangers of the sea. Sightings of the giant squid might have inspired these tales.

▶ Mistaken for a monster! The 15 metre–long giant squid has eyes as big as dinner plates.

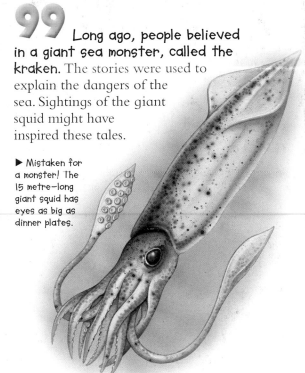

98 The Greek goddess of love was born in the sea. Aphrodite, said to be the daughter of Zeus, was born out of the foam of the sea. The Romans based their love goddess, Venus, on the same story. Lots of artists have painted her rising from the waves in a giant clam shell.

100 Mermaids lured sailors to their deaths on the rocks. Mythical mermaids were said to be half-woman, half-fish. Folklore tells how the mermaids confused sailors with their beautiful singing – with the result that their ships were wrecked on the rocks.

▼ Mermaids were said to have a fishy tail instead of legs.

I DON'T BELIEVE IT!
A mermaid's purse is the name given to the eggcases of the dog shark. They look a little bit like handbags!

Index

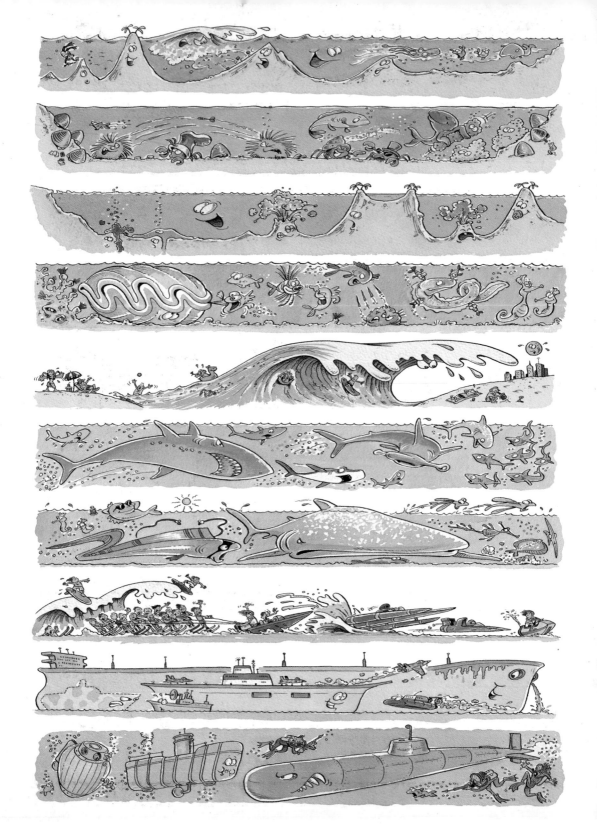